Longman Structural Reader
Stage 2

Ireland

Patrick Tolfree

Longman Group UK Limited,
Longman House, Burnt Mill, Harlow,
Essex CM20 2JE, England
and Associated Companies throughout the world.

© Longman Group UK Limited 1990
All rights reserved; no part of this publication
may be reproduced, stored in a retrieval system,
or transmitted in any form or by any means, electronic,
mechanical, photocopying, recording, or otherwise,
without the prior written permission of the Publishers.

First published 1990

Set in 11/13pt Plantin
Produced by Longman Group (FE) Ltd
Printed in Hong Kong.

ISBN 0582 02574.5

Acknowledgements

We should like to thank the following for permission to use copyright photographs:

Allsport UK Ltd/Billy Stickland for page 43 (right), /Gerard Vandystadt for page 45 (right). Camera Press Ltd for pages 27, 35 (left), 36 and 42. The J Allan Cash Photo Library Ltd for pages 8 (bottom), 9 (top), 12, 19 (right), 20, 21 (top), 21 (bottom), 24, 29 and 31. Ron and Christine Foord for page 31 (insert). The John Hillelson Agency Ltd for page 48 (right). The Hulton-Deutsch Collection Ltd for pages 23, 41 and 47. Impact Photos/ Geray Sweeney for pages 19 (left), 34 and 37. Popperfoto for pages 22 and 48 (left). SDB Media/Eddie for page 46. The Slide File for pages 6 (left), 6 (right), 7, 8 (top), 9 (bottom), 10–11, 13 (top), 13 (bottom), 14 (top), 14 (bottom), 14 (bottom inset), 16, 18, 25, 26 (top), 35 (right), 38, 43 (left), 44 (left), 44 (right). Sporting Pictures (UK) Ltd for pages 45 (left). The Telegraph Colour Library for page 40. Trinity College Library Dublin for pages 15 and 17. Ulster Folk and Transport Museum for page 26 (bottom). Viewfinder Colour Library for page 5. Waterford Crystal for page 30. Zefa Picture Library for page 32.
"Guinness is Good For You", advert on page 28, reproduced with the kind permission of Guiness Brewing G.B.

Cover Photograph by The Slide File.

We are unable to trace the copyright holder of the picture on page 3, and would appreciate any information which would enable us to do so.

Contents

	Page
The Emerald Isle	5
Dublin	12
Irish history and the Church	19
Industry	25
Music	32
Language and literature	38
Sport	43
The Irish abroad	46

The Emerald Isle

Ireland is an island on the west side of Europe. It is a little smaller than Portugal and a little bigger than Sri Lanka.

The country is in two parts. The larger part, the Republic of Ireland, is in the south. There are about 3.5 million people in the Republic of Ireland and its capital city is Dublin. The smaller part of Ireland, Northern Ireland, is part of the United Kingdom and its big city is Belfast. There are about 1.6 million people in Northern Ireland.

Ireland is a small country, but a lot of people in the world know about it. In many countries there are Irish priests and nuns. In many countries there are families which went there from Ireland in the past. They left Ireland to find work in those countries and they stayed there. All over the world there are people with Irish blood. They belong to another country, but Ireland is still, in their heart, their home.

Ireland has never been a very rich country. It is not rich in money, but it is very rich in other things, in music, in poetry, in song.

A village street in Dalin, County Clare

Killary Harbour, County Mayo   *Killary, County Galway*

Like a lot of other countries, Ireland has had sad and difficult times, but it has had good times too. The Irish are kind and friendly people. They welcome strangers, and so a lot of tourists visit Ireland and enjoy it. The Irish love to talk. They are good at conversation. They like to tell funny stories. Perhaps when they tell funny stories they can forget the difficult times.

Ireland is a beautiful country, with fine lakes, tall mountains and attractive beaches. It has two great rivers. One, the Liffey, goes into the sea on the east coast. The other, the Shannon, goes into the sea on the west coast.

It is a very green country. On a tour of Ireland you see a lot of farms and not many factories. Ireland is green partly because it rains so much! Because it is so green, people call it the "Emerald Isle".

Gotahork, County Donegal

*Dingle Peninsula,
County Kerry*

*The Cliffs of Moher,
County Clare*

*Glenariff,
County Antrim*

*Dunamase,
County Laois*

A farm at Slea Head, County Kerry

Dublin

Dublin is on the east coast of Ireland. It is a fine city, with beautiful grey stone houses. The river Liffey runs through the middle and, like London and Paris, Dublin has lots of bridges. Many people know about O'Connell Bridge. It is unusual because it is almost square (47 metres wide and 49 metres across). People know about the Dublin Post Office too. In 1916 there was fighting there between Irishmen and British soldiers.

Because Dublin is near the sea you can sometimes feel the wind on your face in the middle of the city. But if you want to be warm, you can drink coffee in one of the many cafés. Or you can drink beer in a pub.

The River Liffey, Dublin

O'Connell Bridge, Dublin

The General Post Office, Dublin

Irish people drink Guinness, a strong dark beer. Irish (or Gaelic) coffee is another interesting dark drink. This is how you make it. First you put very hot coffee in a glass, with some brown sugar. Then you add whiskey. Then very carefully you add some cream, which stays on top of the whiskey and coffee. It is a very good way to drink whiskey!

Phoenix Park, Dublin; (inset) *deer in Phoenix Park*

A page from The Book of Kells

If you go to Dublin, you must visit Phoenix Park. It has beautiful gardens with deer, and there is a market there on Sundays. There is also horse racing in the park.

When Pope John Paul II visited Ireland in 1979, over one million people came to see and hear him in Phoenix Park.

You must also visit Trinity College. You can see the *Book of Kells* there. It is a very beautiful book. Perhaps there is not a more beautiful book in the world. Irish monks wrote it and painted its pictures 1,200 years ago. It tells the gospel story.

In Trinity College you can also see the Brian Boru Harp. Brian Boru was once king of Ireland, and the harp is very old. The harp was probably made in the 14th century, and Brian Boru lived three hundred years – three centuries – before that. But people have always called it his harp.

Dublin has always been a city of music. The first performance of Handel's *Messiah*, on 17th April 1742, was in Dublin. Because the Irish people liked his music so much, Handel went back to Ireland two or three times after that.

There is a sad and beautiful old song about a Dublin girl, Mollie Malone. She sold shellfish in the streets of Dublin – her father and mother did the same thing before her. The shellfish were cockles and mussels. When she was still young she became ill and died, but her ghost lived after her. The writer of the song does not use the word "love", but he calls her "sweet Mollie Malone", so probably he loved her.

Trinity College, Dublin

The Brian Boru Harp

The statue of Molly Malone, Dublin

Cockles and Mussels

In Dublin's fair city, where the girls are so pretty,
I first set my eyes on sweet Mollie Malone,
As she wheeled her wheelbarrow through streets broad and narrow,
Crying, "Cockles and mussels: alive, alive O!"

She was a fishmonger, but sure 'twas no wonder,
For so were her father and mother before;
They wheeled a wheelbarrow through streets broad and narrow,
Crying, "Cockles and mussels: alive, alive O!"

She died of a fever, and no one could save her,
And that was the end of sweet Mollie Malone,
Now a ghost wheels her barrow through streets broad and narrow,
Crying, "Cockles and mussels: alive, alive O!"

Irish history and the Church

To understand Irish history you must know something about the Irish Church.

Saint Patrick took Christianity to Ireland. Patrick was born in England in about the year 385. When he was about ten years old, some men caught him and took him to Ireland as a slave. He had to look after sheep there. At last, when he was a young man he ran away and went to Europe. There he became a priest, but he always wanted to return to Ireland. When he was about fifty, in the year 432, he went back to the country. He was now a bishop, and he began to convert the people.

A Celtic cross

The churchyard at Glendalough, Wicklow

Patrick walked round the country and talked to the kings and other leaders. The people of Ireland were ready to become Christians, but he had to convert the leaders first. After seven years, Patrick needed three other bishops to help him. He built more than fifty churches in Ireland.

For the next six or seven hundred years, Ireland had fewer wars than many other countries in Europe. This was partly because Patrick left behind him a strong Christian country.

St Patrick's Cross, Cashel, Tipperary

St Patrick's Cathedral

The faith that Patrick gave to the Irish was the Roman Catholic faith. It is still strong there today. Because their faith is so strong, Irish people have been ready to fight for it. So a lot of the history of Ireland is the history of the fight for its faith. If you do not understand that, you cannot understand Ireland today.

St Patrick's grave

A shrine in Blackwater Village, County Wexford

The Norman king of England began, in 1167, to bring Ireland under English rule. But it was hard for England to rule Ireland. Ireland was larger than either Scotland or Wales. There was sea between Ireland and England.

In 1541 Henry VIII, king of England, said that he was king of Ireland. England was not in the Roman Catholic Church. Henry took England out of the Roman Catholic Church when he wanted to divorce his queen, Catherine of Aragon. The Roman Catholic Church was against divorce. So England became a Protestant country, but Ireland did not. When England became Protestant, Ireland became even harder to rule.

Queen Elizabeth I was the daughter of Henry VIII. Elizabeth's soldiers beat an Irish army at the battle of Kinsale in 1601 and brought Protestants into the country. The Protestants who went to Ireland from England were called settlers. The settlers were stronger in the north of Ireland than in the south.

The Irish Catholics did not want to become Protestant and they hated the Protestant settlers. For many years there was fighting between the English and the Irish. Then in 1642 the army of Oliver Cromwell ended the rebellion. But the Irish did not change their faith. The Protestants were strong only in the north.

Cromwell's attack on Drogheda, 1649

A Royal Mail van set on fire during rioting in Belfast

From 1801 there were Irish representatives in the British Parliament. At first only Protestants could represent Ireland as Members of Parliament (MPs). After 1829 there were some Catholic MPs. But during the nineteenth century, more and more people in Ireland wanted the country to become independent.

The road to independence was long and painful. In 1921, after rebellions, demonstrations and war, the larger, southern part of the country became the Irish Free State. Northern Ireland was still part of Great Britain.

There are still terrible problems in Ireland. About two-thirds of the people in Northern Ireland are Protestants and about one third are Catholics. In the south almost all the people are Catholic. Some people in both the north and the south want Ireland to be one country, and since 1969 there has been fighting and killing. People are still trying to find a way of ending these difficulties.

Industry

Ireland is a country of good butter, good beer and good horses. People come from all over the world to buy Irish horses, from Europe, from America, from Arab countries and from the Far East.

Ireland also has its manufacturing industry. For 300 years there have been factories which make linen. Nearly all of them are in the north. Today there are factories making pharmaceutical products and computers and other modern products.

A horse fair

A modern industrial estate near Dublin

A nineteenth century linen factory

The sinking of the Titanic, *1912*

For over one and a half centuries, Belfast has built ships. The *Titanic* was built there in 1912. On its first voyage, from England to America, the *Titanic* hit an iceberg and sank, 1,513 people lost their lives and only a few hundred were saved.

Guinness

People in all parts of the world know the name of Guinness. It is a kind of beer. Another name for it is "stout". It is different from all other beers, with its dark brown, almost black colour, and its white, creamy head.

Guinness is made from barley, hops, yeast and water. Everything in it is quite natural; there are no chemicals. They have made, or "brewed", it in Dublin since 1759. The

first man to make it was Arthur Guinness. Beer is made in a brewery. The Guinness brewery in Dublin is bigger than any other brewery in Europe.

Today there are also Guinness breweries in Britain, Nigeria, Malaysia, Cameroun and Ghana. It is sold in 134 countries of the world, from A to Z – from Algeria, Argentina and Australia to Zaire and Zambia. People drink more than seven million glasses of Guinness every day around the world!

Guinness advertisements are well known. The first advertisement, in 1929, was "Guinness is good for you".

Guinness is also good for Ireland. 4,500 people work for Guinness itself, and the jobs of 30,000 others come from it. The barley that goes into Guinness is grown on Irish farms. People also say that the water of the river Liffey helps to make the Guinness brewed in Dublin good.

There are some good stories about Guinness. One is about an officer who fought in the Battle of Waterloo in 1815. He was wounded, but he drank a bottle of Guinness every day and got better!

Writers like Dickens, R.L. Stevenson and James Joyce brought Guinness into their writing. James Joyce called it "the wine of the country".

Whiskey

Ireland has its own whiskey. It probably started with the monks who came to Ireland from the continent of Europe in the fifth and sixth centuries. They knew a lot about the way to make spirits. From them the Irish learned to make whiskey.

Irish whiskey is made differently from Scotch whisky. It is also usually spelled differently – Scotch whisky has no "e". Irish whiskey tastes lighter and smoother than Scotch whisky. Some people like Scotch whisky, and some like Irish whiskey. Just now more people in the world drink Scotch whisky.

People "brew" beer, but whiskey is "distilled". It is made in a distillery. At one time there were hundreds of small

Bottling at Bushmills Distillery, the world's oldest distillery

distilleries in Ireland. This was not good for the Irish economy. Now there are only two distilleries, and Ireland is beginning to sell more of its whiskey outside Ireland.

In the American Civil War someone said to President Lincoln that General Ulysses S. Grant was drinking too much Irish whiskey. Lincoln knew that Grant was a good general, and he knew that Irish whiskey was a good drink. So Lincoln's answer was: "Find out the make of General Grant's whiskey. Then give it to the other generals!"

Waterford glass

One fine thing that Ireland makes is Waterford glass, or crystal. Waterford is in the south east of Ireland.

Waterford glass was famous in the last century, but in the early part of this century people nearly forgot the way to make it. Then in 1951 a man called Joe McGrath started a company which brought back the art and gave people work. The company, Waterford Crystal, has grown. It makes most beautiful crystal products and they are sold in every part of the world.

Glass engraving at Waterford Crystal

An Aer Lingus plane with (inset) *shamrock*

Aer Lingus

If you go to Ireland by aeroplane, perhaps you will travel by the Irish airline, Aer Lingus. The Aer Lingus company belongs to the Irish state. It is a large, very successful airline, and it takes passengers to and from very many countries in the world. Many people know the green Aer Lingus emblem. It is a shamrock – the shape of a pretty little Irish plant.

Aer Lingus does not only fly planes. For example, it has a hotel in New York and a hospital in Baghdad.

Music

Ireland is strong and rich in music. The Irish people love to sing, to dance and to make music of all kinds.

The harp

The harp has always been a very important musical instrument in Ireland. In the seventeenth century it became more than that. In the wars between the Irish and the English, the harp was like a national flag for the Irish. Queen Elizabeth knew that. After the battle of Kinsale in 1601, she ordered her army to kill all harpers. Cromwell's army, too, treated harpers very badly. The soldiers often burned them. From that time the harp has been a national emblem.

O'Carolan

One very famous Irish harper was Turlogh O'Carolan. O'Carolan was born in Westmeath in about 1670. When he was about sixteen years old, his eyes failed and he became

Playing the harp

blind. With the help of a kind, rich lady, Mrs MacDermott Roe, he learned to play the harp. Mrs Roe gave the blind harper a horse and a guide, and for fifty years he went round the country and played the harp for a living. He also wrote poetry and music for the harp. People have saved a lot of his music, and harpers still play O'Carolan's beautiful songs.

When O'Carolan was an old man, he went back to the house of Mrs MacDermott Roe. On his death-bed he took up his harp for the last time and played *O'Carolan's Farewell to Music*. People from every part of Ireland came to his funeral.

Thomas Moore

In the early nineteenth century Thomas Moore wrote a song called *The Harp that once through Tara's Halls*. That is the first line of the song. Tara is where the kings of Ireland once lived. In this song Tara is another name for Ireland.

In the song, Moore calls the music of the harp the "soul of music". At one time, people heard the music of the harp everywhere in Ireland, but now no one plays the harp. It hangs on the walls without a sound – "mute" Moore calls it. The Irish cannot now feel in their hearts the pride and glory of the old days. Pride "sleeps" and the "thrill" of glory has gone. Perhaps, Moore thinks, the pride of Ireland will one day wake again.

> The harp that once through Tara's halls,
> The soul of music shed,
> Now hangs as mute on Tara's walls
> As if that soul were fled.
>
> So sleeps the pride of former days,
> So glory's thrill is o'er,
> And hearts, that once beat high for praise,
> Now feel that pulse no more!

Children at a dancing contest

Thomas Moore wrote other songs: *Love Thee, Dearest, The Last Rose of Summer* and *The Meeting of the Waters*. A great Irish singer, John McCormack (1884–1945), made them famous in America. They made Irish Americans remember their country.

The harp is not now the main musical instrument in Ireland. Irish pipes and the violin have taken its place. Irish people play them for dances like the jig, the hornpipe and the reel. These dances have a quick, strong rhythm and they need a lot of energy. They are still popular today.

John Field

When they hear the word "nocturne", people usually think of Chopin. Chopin's nocturnes are famous, but the first nocturnes came from an Irishman. He was John Field, and he was born in Dublin in 1782, the son of a violin player. He was a pupil in London of the great piano player, composer and teacher Clementi. "Perhaps Beethoven is the best piano player in the world," people said in the early nineteenth century, "but Field is surely the next best." He was one of the really great pianists.

We can't hear him today because there were no records of music in his time. But he has left some very beautiful nocturnes that will give pleasure for a long time.

Today there are many fine Irish musicians. A lot of them are internationally famous, and that is wonderful for a country with only five million people. The world knows the flute player James Galway, the singer Bernadette Greery, the violinist Geraldine O'Grade, the organist Gerard Gillen, the pianist John O'Conor – and many others.

Ireland also has its great pop and rock musicians.

Bob Geldof

In the early 1980s Bob Geldof and the Boomtown Rats were famous for songs like *Rat Trap, Looking After Number One* and *I Don't Like Mondays*. They were part of the "new wave" of punk music. The group toured America and were very successful.

Bob Geldof does not dress very well. He does not comb his hair much. He does not shave very often. He says terrible things. Bob Geldof is a great man.

Bob Geldof

James Galway

In 1984 there was a famine in Ethiopia – thousands of people died because there was not enough food. Bob Geldof wanted to help them. First, with Midge Ure, he wrote a song: *Do they know it's Christmas?* Then Bob Geldof and some of the great pop artists of the world made a record of the song. People bought more copies than any record in history. The money from that very successful record went to help the people of Ethiopia.

Then in 1985 Bob Geldof organised two "Live Aid" concerts. One was in London, the other in Philadelphia. They were at the same time and people in 500 million homes saw the concerts on TV. The idea was to make money for Ethiopia. People gave £100,000,000. There has never been anything like it.

U2

Another very successful pop group is U2. The group started in Dublin in 1979. U2 is a rock group, and the words of their songs are very important. The group know the young people of Ireland and the things that they feel and want. They speak for young Irish people, but they are famous all over the world.

U2

The Chieftains

The Chieftains

The Chieftains are Irish – really Irish. The group began in 1963. They play the old music of Ireland, and they use the old instruments – the violin, the pipes, the flute, the harp. They make music that is magic. In 1975 they gave a concert at the Albert Hall in London. It was 17th March, Saint Patrick's Day, the most important day in the year for the Irish. 6,000 people came to the concert. They came just to listen, but the music was so strong, so beautiful, so magic that they began to dance.

There are six musicians in the group. Their sizes are so different that it is difficult to put them in the same photograph. But that doesn't matter. It is their music that matters, and they play the music of Ireland.

Language and literature

The Irish have their own language. It comes from their Celtic history. But today, out of about five million people in the whole of the country, only 50,000 still speak it. Nearly all Irish people speak English.

The Irish speak English in their own special way. Foreigners don't easily understand an Irish accent, but it is strong and musical, and many people think that it is very attractive. The accent in the north of the country is different from the accent in the south, but a foreigner can't easily hear the difference.

Many fine writers have come from Ireland. Some, like W.B. Yeats and James Joyce, have helped the world to know Ireland better. Those two writers were writing at the end of the last century and the beginning of this one, when Ireland was on the road to independence. They understood their country well, and so, in their writing, they made others understand it too.

The Isle of Innisfree

W.B. Yeats (1865–1939)

W.B. Yeats wrote both plays and poems, but we remember him as a poet, maybe the greatest Irish poet ever. One of his very beautiful poems is "The Lake Isle of Innisfree". Innisfree is an island on a lake in a far-away part of north-west Ireland.

The poet is saying that he wants to go there for a quiet, peaceful life. He will build a small house and grow his own vegetables. The only noise will be the sounds of nature: the crickets, the wings of birds and the water of the lake. He is writing the poem in some grey city, but he hears the sounds of the lake deep in his heart.

The Lake Isle of Innisfree

I will arise and go now, and go to Innisfree,
And a small cabin build there, of clay and wattles made;
Nine bean rows will I have there, a hive for the honey bee,
And live alone in the bee-loud glade.

And I shall have some peace there, for peace comes dropping slow,
Dropping from the veils of morn to where the cricket sings;
There midnight's all a-glimmer, and noon a purple glow,
And evening full of the linnet's wings.

I will arise and go now, for always night and day
I hear lake water lapping with low sounds by the shore;
While I stand on the roadway, or on the pavements gray,
I hear it in the deep heart's core.

A lot of people remember the line "Nine bean rows will I have there, a hive for the honey bee". Why *nine* rows of beans?

James Joyce, drawn by a pavement artist

James Joyce (1882–1942)

James Joyce was the first of ten children. He was born near Dublin. He went to school and college in Dublin, but when he was still a young man he went to live in Paris. For many years of his life he was in Paris, Italy or Switzerland, but his books were about Ireland. For his first book, *Dubliners*, he wrote short stories about his time as a boy in Dublin. His best known book is *Ulysses*, also about Dublin. *Ulysses* tells the story of twenty-four hours in the life of three Dublin people, Stephen Dedalus, Leopold Bloom and his wife Molly. The book gives us all the things they did or thought that day. There was never a book like *Ulysses* before. It is one of the really important books of the twentieth century.

There are some famous Irish writers like Oscar Wilde and G.B. Shaw who did not write about Ireland.

Oscar Wilde (1854–1900)

Oscar Wilde was born in Dublin. He went to Trinity College, Dublin, and later to Oxford University. Wilde wrote novels and poetry but people remember his plays.

Oscar Wilde was a very witty man. He could make people laugh. Most of his plays are comedies. *Lady Windermere's Fan*, *A Woman of No Importance* and *The Importance of Being Earnest* are comedies that we still laugh at.

Here are two sayings from his plays:

"All women become like their mothers. That is their tragedy. No man does. That is his."

"Children begin by loving their parents. After a time they judge them. Rarely, if ever, do they forgive them."

When Oscar Wilde went through the customs in New York, he said "I have nothing to declare except my genius."

Oscar Wilde

George Bernard Shaw

George Bernard Shaw (1856–1950)

G.B. Shaw was also born in Dublin and also wrote plays. Like Wilde, Shaw was a very witty man, but he was above all a thinker. He wanted to change the things that were wrong in the world. He disliked the things that were false.

At one time, people thought that Shaw was a second William Shakespeare. Today, in the last years of the twentieth century, not many people think that, but a lot of people go to see his plays. Three very famous plays are *Arms and the Man*, *Saint Joan* and *Pygmalion*.

Here are two sayings from his plays:

"He who can, does. He who cannot, teaches."

"Liberty means responsibility. That is why most people dread it."

Sport

The Irish play football and rugby football, but they also have their own games: hurling and Gaelic football.

Hurling is played with a stick like a hockey stick. The ball, a *sliothar*, is very small and you can hit it very far. It is a very fast game, and very exciting to watch. Perhaps there is not a faster game in the world. Hurling is played all over Ireland, like baseball in America or cricket in England. Nearly every Irish town has its own team, and every year there is a competition to find the best team in the country. The final, usually very exciting, is played at Croke Park in Dublin. 70,000 people watch it.

Gaelic football is played with a ball like a soccer ball. The players can both kick the ball and touch it with their hands. There are fifteen players on each side. Teams play Gaelic football all over the country, and there is a competition each year to find which is the best team.

The horse

Ireland is a good country for horses because the grass is green and sweet and there is a lot of it.

Irish race horses are famous all over the world. A lot of the Irish jockeys that ride the horses are famous too. They ride

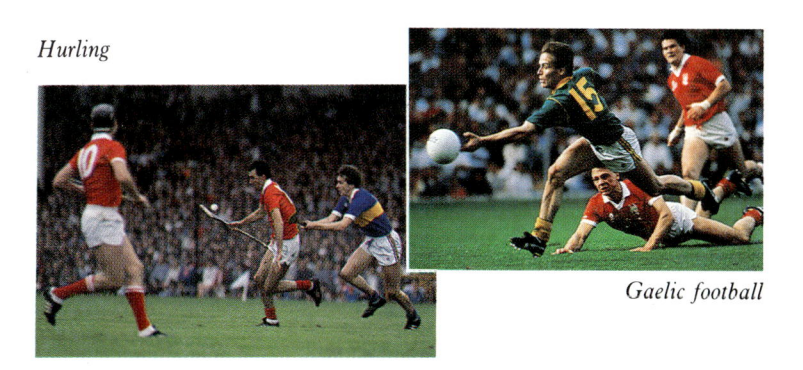

Hurling

Gaelic football

Race horses

not only in Ireland. You can see them on racecourses in many parts of the world. There are a lot of great Irish jockeys like Jonjo O'Neill, Pat Taafe and Pat Eddery. Some jockeys become trainers when they are older. They train the horses that the jockeys ride. Perhaps you know the name of one famous Irish trainer – Vincent O'Brien. But people love and remember the horses best – Irish horses like Arkle, Prince Regent, Dawn Run and Nijinski.

The Irish people love to go to the races. Horse racing brings colour and excitement to people's lives. For most of the year there are races in different parts of the country. The most important race of the year is the Irish Sweeps Derby at the Curragh, and there are summer race festivals at Galway, Tralee, Killarney, Listowel and Tramore.

Barry McGuigan

Many great boxers have come from Ireland. On 8th June 1985, Barry McGuigan from Northern Ireland beat Eusabio Pedrosa from Panama in Belfast, in the fight for featherweight championship of the world. McGuigan won the fight and his victory brought Catholics and Protestants together. Later Catholics and Protestants travelled together to watch him fight in London. When he stepped into the ring people saw that on his robe there was a dove of peace.

Stephen Roche

In 1987 an Irishman won the most important cycle race in the world, the Tour de France. His name was Stephen Roche. The Prime Minister of Ireland, Mr Charles Haughey, went to Paris to meet him when he finished the race, to say "Well done!" After the race Stephen Roche returned to Dublin, his home town, and 20,000 people came out to welcome him and to cheer him.

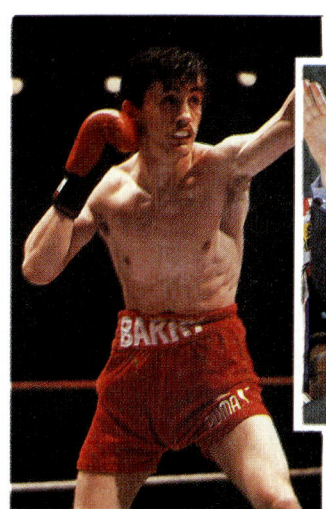

Barry McGuigan

Stephen Roche with Charles Haughey after winning the Tour de France

The Irish abroad

All over the world today there are people who came from Ireland. Very many more people are glad to say: "My family once came from Ireland." Their parents, their grandparents or their great-grandparents were Irish.

People have left Ireland for lots of different reasons.

After Ireland became Christian in the fifth century, Irish monks and scholars left the country to teach the word of God. They went particularly to the cities of Europe – to Kiev in Russia, to Lucca in Italy, to Iona in Scotland. Since then Ireland has continued to send missionaries round the world – nuns and priests and others. They take their faith to other countries, as Saint Patrick took Christianity to Ireland. Today there are 5,000 Irish missionaries in eighty-six different countries. Many people first learn English from the Irish nuns who are teachers in their country.

From the beginning of the seventeenth century the English Protestants made life very difficult for the Irish Catholics. Catholics could not buy land. They could not do any of the public jobs. They could not become soldiers. Because of these difficulties many Irish people left the

An Irish nun teaching English

Poor Irish peasants searching for potatoes

country. They went to start a new life in some other country. Many became soldiers for other Catholic countries. They hoped that perhaps those countries would help throw the English Protestants out of Ireland.

Very many people have left Ireland to look for work. Ireland is a small country. Often there are not enough jobs for everyone.

Many people left Ireland in the middle of the last century in the Great Famine. In the early years of the century potatoes were almost the only food in the country. Then in the 1840s there was a potato famine. The potatoes did not grow. In 1847 and 1848 there were no potatoes at all. Many people were terribly hungry in the Great Famine, many died

Irish Americans celebrating St Patrick's day in New York

President Kennedy with his wife and parents

and many left the country to go to Britain, Canada, the USA and other countries. The number of people in the country went down from eight to six million.

Today, over forty million people in the USA say that they have some Irish blood. The families of President J.F. Kennedy, President Richard Nixon and President Ronald Reagan were once Irish. President Kennedy was the first Catholic President of the USA.

Nearly 30 per cent of Australians have Irish blood. Between 1929 and 1949 six of the seven Australian prime ministers were from Irish families.

The first prime minister of New Zealand, John Edward Fitzgerald, was born in Ireland. Today, 15 per cent of New Zealanders have some Irish blood.

The people who leave Ireland do not forget it. Their children, and their children's children do not forget it either. In their "deep heart's core" many of them would like to return to Ireland.